Time Junkie

101 Ways for Business Owners to Break the Habit and Get More Free Time NOW!

by Andrea Feinberg

D1564144

> *" The secret to life is enjoying the passage of time "*
>
> *James Taylor*

Published by Coaching Insight LLC

Dedication

Dedicated to my husband, Marshall, whose 100% support gave me the time to get this done and with whom the Zone is a lot more fun.

A warm 'thank you' to the clients, friends, mentors and colleagues whose stories, candor and perspective gave me the opportunity to learn these many lessons on building a healthy business for a healthy, happy life.

With love and gratitude to my mom, Beverly who raised me right; to my sister, Robin who remembers absolutely everything; and to absent friends and family whose memories add a smile to my face.

About the Author

A ndrea Feinberg, M.B.A., C.P.B.A., is President of Coaching Insight, LLC, which identifies and leverages underused assets for small business owners. As a Wall Street executive, wholesale business owner, marketing consultant, and coach, Andrea has decades of experience helping clients articulate, achieve and exceed their goals, whether for business or their personal lives. The key to her action-oriented business process is a simple yet powerful concept - how we respond to the realities and circumstances of our businesses has a fundamental impact on what those realities and circumstances are. Clients have included Standard & Poor's Corporation, Integ, Sandler Sales Institute, Cameron Advertising, The Marketing Resource Group, Provista Group, KMF Property Management, Certified Payroll, and others.

Andrea is a certified facilitator for The Alternative Board, a certified mentor for EQMentor.com and the Small Business Expert on LongIsland.com. She's held a variety of roles in her local business community including Vice Chair, Brookhaven's Small Business Advisory Council; President, Westbury Chamber of Commerce, and adjunct instructor for Hofstra University. She has been profiled in The New York Times, Newsday, and Long Island Business News; published in "Business to Business Magazine", "Creations Magazine", 'The Hauppauge Reporter", "Generations Magazine" and many online publications. In 2004, she collaborated on an award-winning book: The Essential Coaching Book.

Until 1988, Andrea was a manager for Standard & Poor's Corporation, with a 10-year success record building a multi-million dollar business unit with a 75% Return On Sales. Over the next 13 years she built a wholesale gift enterprise that she subsequently sold and embarked on training for her professional coach designation.

She is a graduate of Coach University's 3-year advanced coach training program, a Founding Member of Coachville and of the International Association of Coaching and is a Certified Strategic Business Leadership Coach. Andrea received her Certified Professional Behavioral Analyst designation from Target Training International, her M.B.A., Marketing, from New York University's Stern School of Business and her B.A. in Anthropology, Hofstra University.

 Note from the Author:

So why the heck should you care about any of that stuff above? Simply this: with all that experience, education and personal development in diverse arenas, I have consistently focused on the small business owner - the good, the bad and the pretty ugly. In fact, I've been one since 1988. Believe me, I really get it. Nothing in these Tips is hard or complicated or 'out-there'. It's all just for you.

I host two main websites, both of which are focused on the concerns and opportunities of small business owners.

Products and conversations that respond specifically to using time effectively on behalf of enjoying a well-run business, a fulfilling life and fewer sleepless nights can be found at

www.morefreetimezone.com

A broader selection of products and services related to marketing, leadership development, effective employee recruiting and training, goal setting and prioritizing can be found at

www.coachinginsight.com

Table of Contents

Introduction 2

How do I Use this Book (I Don't Have a Lot of Time) 12

Chapter 1: Having a Life 16

Chapter 2: A Little Personal Development 24

Chapter 3: Now, Let's Take Care of Business 36

Just One More Thing 64

Appendix: Mind Benders for New Perspective 68

Other Valuable Resources from Andrea Feinberg
to Have More Money, Enjoy Your Business
and Love Your Life 78

Claim your free gift valued at $ 250.00 here: www.morefreetimezone.com/gift

Introduction

S ince 1999, I've coached hundreds of business owners and there's been a constant theme every one of them has shared with me: a desire to have more free time - time with family and friends; time to pursue more money and, ultimately, freedom. I wouldn't be surprised if having more free time is your dream too.

Having free time is the great reward that represents freedom. Sure, having money earned from a well-run and successful enterprise is certainly a joy; it provides for so much that's good in life. Yet many business owners find that they can't get to the true money-making endeavors without access to more free time – it's the key to having more money, to enjoying business and loving life. Even so, it's a confounding blessing; we love having more but there's just no more to be had. It's non-renewable and no 'do-overs' are allowed.

Where does more free time come from? Can't buy it on Amazon, there are no auctions for it on Ebay and even Bloomingdales doesn't have a department for it. No - enjoying more free time comes from having systems, having your priorities guide your decisions and tasks; more free time comes from recognizing that speeding up to get more done in less time won't get you to your vision of success. What is that vision? Is it the freedom to direct yourself in any of hundreds of imagined pleasurable ways? Is it the opportunity to finally pursue the true money-making ventures you don't have time to develop now? Is it the opportunity to simply enjoy the company of those you love and who love you? However the reward of more free time touches you, it's this sublime state that I call living in the 'More Free Time Zone'. No matter what it says on your clock in your part of the world you're completely in control of your daily 24-hour cycle. The More Free Time Zone is, as James Taylor sings, 'enjoying the passage of time' with the experiences, joys and success that surround you.

More than any other desire or imagined goal, this is what I've heard from every business owner I've worked with in more than a decade as a professional coach. They all want this one thing: more free time to enjoy in ways they haven't been able to find from working. And sometimes, they want more free time simply to build the larger framework for their growing business, something they can't seem to do while so vitally engaged in the day-to-day running and crisis management of their current situation.

Ironically, more free time is what many of them are in the market to gain with the sale of their business; as the first baby boomers turn 65, it's estimated that more than 8 million businesses will be put up for sale. And yet, if those owners are still intrinsically a part of their company's business proposition – if they're the key element that makes the business work, if they believe 'I AM the business', if a day away would cripple operations and opportunities – then they're literally diminishing the value of their enterprise.

Why? Think about it: when you sell the business, if you and your over-stuffed head full of relationships, processes, deals, decision-making and reputation are the primary assets of the enterprise, just what do you think you're selling? How will you walk away from your business if you have to stick around to transfer all its value and fundamental knowledge to a new owner? How will the potential buyer be able to envision their own success if they will have to continue to rely on you to make it happen?

And so, you see, there are two critical reasons for every business owner to find more free time – probably more if we add in your very personal reasons for wanting it. Don't gloss over those two points; they'll have a huge impact on all the years you spend building your business and the pleasure you can enjoy after you sell it. So let me say it this way: This is my core message in every program I deliver and every coaching conversation I have:

1 Without more free time to pursue the big picture needs of your business, your family, your life, how will you ever do the work that no one else is capable of doing? Who will build the vision, relationships, alliances, reputation and strategies if you don't have time to get them done?

2 Without more free time that comes from letting go of so much of your daily business responsibilities, how will you truly maximize the value of your business and enjoy its great reward? Who will want to buy a business that resides in your head and not in the intrinsic processes and successes of the business itself?

The point here is that you CAN build a business that's consistent with and honors your priorities, values and goals. Of course, it's important to know what those are. However, unless you take the time to follow that imperative, you're adding unnecessary grey hair, ulcers and sleepless nights and I've yet to meet anyone for whom that's a goal. So, use this book to find just one more way - with more free time - to ensure you're always focused on the big picture of your life.

Your business exists within the context of your life. Too many business owners make the mistake of believing the reverse and lose out on a treasure of experience, wealth, love and personal abundance. Don't think you have to alter your life, your family, friendships and plans to conform to the runaway monster of your business. Do the reverse: tame the monster and make it your servant. Having the time to plan for just this is part of what you'll gain from the Tips in this book. And then, having achieved that new business environment, you'll have all the time to enjoy the More Free Time Zone, whether to build the next enterprise or just to enjoy the sun on your face without concern for what has to be done tomorrow.

From all the many years that my clients have let me in to their lives and dreams, and from hundreds of hours of conversation, a series of steps emerged, steps that enabled clients to move beyond their roadblocks and struggles. Steps that helped them re-shape their response to time. Ideas to help create their personally held dreams: having more choice, having more growth, enjoying the freedom and security represented by having more money. **And it all came out achieving this one goal: having more free time.**

If you want to maximize the value of your business and position its assets as valuable to your future buyer, then you'd better get out of the way. Showing you how to transfer most of the daily responsibilities to a well-trained staff is an important benefit you'll get from this book and its companion tools at

www.morefreetimezone.com

Is this book for you? Yes – it's for you if you have the commitment to make serious changes in the daily routine of your life and the way you run your business and if you recognize you're the only one who can make those changes. It's for you if you want a bit of help learning specific steps you can take, day by day, to enjoy the reward of one hour more every week; an hour's gift to use as you wish. **One hour a week that will grow into the choice, freedom or financial independence you'll subsequently pursue and enjoy, with all the accumulated hours to come. And, they will come.**

As a result of following through on the suggestions in this book, you'll find precious new blocks of time to build your business, to enjoy your life. How will you capitalize on an hour here or two hours there? The time itself may be all you want, the reward you seek. Or you may want to find ways to use the time in higher level activity than you've done in the past: envisioning, strategizing, developing new company leaders and planning business development. In the back of the book I've listed some additional products you may find relevant as you build the time to focus on bigger picture thinking for yourself and your business. But later - don't get distracted now. We've got work to focus on right now and focus is one of the steps we're going to employ on your journey to your More Free Time Zone.

Let me start by telling you the principles that have directed development of this program. They're guiding principles that imbue all my work. They're important tools that will help you discover other options and perspectives than the ones you may have considered so far; and finding new options is the way to find more free time.

The best choices are those that come from a sense of self-awareness. When we choose with other people's perspectives in mind; when we conclude without examining the evidence of our own gut; when we respond to others' values and priorities without concern for our own, self-awareness suffers. Having self-awareness is a basic, foundational component you must have to move forward in a way that best suits you. Without this, you're always second-guessing the rightness of your decisions.

Tools are meant to serve a purpose; they're nothing if you don't use them. The tips, suggestions, exercises and ideas here are interesting and, I hope, even provocative. So what? They have no true value until used and put to service in a way that will be practical for you; there's no real reward unless you follow through to create the results you want. I can't reach through the book and do the work for you! It's only when tools are used and concepts are applied to real needs that their power is revealed.

The reason the personal development industry is a multi-billion dollar one, and growing, is because people keep spending money, hoping to find answers to their problems and prayers in gurus, cds, books, seminars, retreats and other engaging techniques.

They're not there. To be sure, wisdom, insights, and new perspectives are to be found in seeking, listening, reading and attending events. Yet the answers and real benefits lie in how you use what you've learned.

Discovery and learning are wonderful motivators; let them motivate you to action! As Napoleon Hill writes in his landmark book Think and Grow Rich: "Knowledge will not attract (anything) unless it is organized and intelligently directed through practical plans of action to the definite end of accumulation of (what you want). Lack of understanding of this fact has been the source of confusion to millions of people who falsely believe that 'knowledge is power.' It is nothing of the sort! Knowledge is only potential power. It becomes power only when, and if, it is organized into definite plans of action and directed to a definite end."

Please – don't spend your money on another product if that's the only investment you plan to make. Invest your time, energy and commitment afterwards and the return for you will be marvelous, I promise.

Guiding Principle #3:

You can manage yourself through the flow of time yet time is not a commodity that can be managed. This is important; too many consultants will try to sell you on managing time. Your experience of time has more to do with your thoughts than a clock and a race. That race is so often filled with anxiety because we make a connection between time and money; in fact, we often say time IS money.

The stress you feel with time is its association with a time-limited opportunity or obligation. A key tool to lift the stress you feel about time is to shift your sense of time from its hold on your thoughts and actions. Recognize that time is a powerful resource and you know everything about it; there are no surprises in seconds, minutes and hours – they're always the same, every day of the week. You've been living with time your entire life. Time is a resource, a partner in your life that, until time travel is on the menu at a spa or department store, will not change. Learn how to use it as it is and not be controlled by it.

Guiding Principle #4:

The key to accepting change is a simple yet powerful concept - how we respond to the realities and circumstances of our life or business has a fundamental impact on WHAT those realities and circumstances are. Be willing to acknowledge that you shape your reality, not by events, rather, by your response to events – every single day. Your life and business are certainly influenced by what others decide or the outside forces you can't control. However, the impact of those decisions and forces is eventually in your control given how you choose to respond to them.

I'm not blind to tragedy, market forces, accident and others' decisions, any of which will have an impact on you. What I'm saying is you have the ability to choose – once you've taken in and considered what has happened. You can choose how you're going to respond to any of these situations, no matter how overwhelming or desperate. Don't confuse 'what may happen' with thinking something has 'happened to you'.

Author and motivational speaker Bob Proctor uses a diagram in his work that shows this so nicely. Imagine a large circle sitting directly above a smaller circle, maybe 1/4 the size of the first one.

The large circle is divided in half: conscious and unconscious mind. The smaller of the two circles is the body. Our mind directs our body by its dominant force in our lives. Our conscious mind can choose to either accept or reject information that comes our way via any of our five senses. However our unconscious mind cannot choose. It takes it all in - information, experiences, images, even lies and misunderstanding - filing it away in a huge store house of available data, to be used to help us with interpretation – interpretation and significance of future events, words, relationships and possibilities. It's important to acknowledge that what we may think is 'independent action' is really pre-determined by what's already in our mind, telling us how to respond to a given event based on past events we've already experienced and stored away.

I'm urging you to recognize this fact and, with conscious effort, evaluate events, life-changing or not, on their own merit and always insert your true free will to guide you toward the best possible outcome, not necessarily the socially or conventionally appropriate one. Remove your emotional response from the event before you make a choice to take action. Recognize that choices are there and you'll always be able to shape the outcome, given the circumstances you must now deal with, no matter what has happened.

Do you want to live in a 'More Free Time Zone'? Visit this one. First, please schedule some daily reading time so it gets done without feeling you're compromising time you'd already set aside for something else. Read the Tips and plan which ones you'll apply first by filling in the lines provided for you so you can take action! They won't all be relevant for you. However, I know that the ones you do choose to apply in your life and business will result in the gift of more free time – time to make more money, enjoy your business and love your life!

Claim your free gift valued at $ 250.00 here: www.morefreetimezone.com/gift

How Do I Use This Book?

I don't have a lot of time...

So glad you asked. There are 3 primary sections here; below the heading for each you'll find a brief client case study that illustrates how the general Tips from that section had an impact for business owners I've coached; it's possible you'll recognize your own situation in any of these brief summaries.

Throughout there are a few standout Tips that require serious thought or mental shift; they may not sit well with you. You'll see them clearly highlighted with an icon of a bookmark. (A key to all icons used in the book is on page 14) These are the recommendations that, in my opinion, will have far-reaching impact for you. Not only will they succeed in opening windows of time for you, they'll also expand they way in which you're likely to approach, evaluate and resolve issues, challenges or opportunities long after you think the impact of this book has run its course. Don't let them go by without getting your full attention.

The sections are:

Having a Life - These are the changes, generally occurring in home or family life, that will pertain to almost anyone; they will be familiar to you as time-consuming tasks that could easily be done in a different way to remove the time constraint they add to your life.

Personal Development - These changes call for a different kind of commitment: those of perspective, attitude, beliefs and assumptions. These form our mental environment and will direct the outcomes and opportunities available to us. Want to expand the range of outcomes or opportunities available to you? Change these first; without a shift in the way you filter and use incoming experience and information, it's impossible to change your actions. And success in business, as in life, is all about your actions.

Let's Take Care of Business - These are the Tips that will relate specifically to a variety of common business situations; the ways in which we misuse time and misinterpret its power over us. Ideas for team development, delegation, training, prioritizing, goal setting, holding effective meetings and self-management are all here.

You may want to pass by the first 2 sections and get right down to business or just read and implement those specific Tips throughout the book that respond to your immediate situation. That's ok; most of the Tips don't rely on each other for greater effectiveness.

However, I AM a business coach and you may find that reflected in the much larger section devoted to business Tips. I know that so much time (often, not very productive) gets sucked away there. Yet, because we don't leave our personal lives at home when we go to work and work tends to come home with us, (even if just in our brains) you'll find that implementing Tips from each section will, over time, have an impact on other areas of life including your health, relationships, financial abundance, spiritual wellness. It's all connected.

The result of the changes you see from each section will be an improved sense of opportunity and self-direction. And, bottom line: more free time with which to implement those opportunities.

Serious about implementing change in your relationship with time? Most of the Tips come with a follow-up question or two. Here's your space to try out an idea, get it on paper and see how it feels. Others are either self-explanatory or require reflection before action. Consider these your opportunity to take action NOW and begin the process for finding more free time a.s.a.p. Here's to finding your More Free Time Zone; so get started - the clock's ticking...

Icons and what they represent:

 This is a 'head's up' moment for you; just slow down, something's coming that could reveal you to yourself.

 Where you see this, please take an extra moment to digest; in what way does the text here relate specifically to your own situation? What's going on for you or what pattern of your own behavior could be improved with application of the suggestion here?

 Implementation of this one Tip could have cascading results, changing far more than is implied in just the brief suggestion printed on the page. Check in with yourself a month after you implement these 'bookmarked' Tips. How much more free time have these Tips provided than any other change you've applied?

Chapter 1

Having a Life

we're starting out easy here

Example of how these Tips could work for you:

Time for Act Two:

My client had been a business owner for over a decade when he came to me. Wanting to start a new enterprise and losing interest in his current one, he saw no way to move forward as he was dependant on his current business to support him and his family. Over time, we discussed ways he could shift his many administrative responsibilities and trust virtual assistants to handle tasks that others could easily take on. He found resources that would do this work capably and within his financial reach. Once these habits began to change, his attention shifted strongly to the new business and within a few months, he launched a new website, wrote a book, and created a series of products all for the new business. And he lived happily ever after.

1

Learn to just say 'no - and thank you for asking me' on a regular basis. This is how we get out of accepting responsibilities that we'll soon resent. Just decide that having been asked is flattery enough - and delight in all the time you don't need to divert to what could have been another responsibility for which you wouldn't get paid.

Who do you know is about to ask you to take on something you really don't want to do?   MCLI,

....

....

What obligation did you accept that has become a burden and you need to let it go?

....

....

2

Buy in bulk. You'll always have reserves on hand - so won't need to do an emergency run for X - and you'll enjoy better pricing.

Which 5 items make sense for you to purchase first?

PRINTER INK ....

....

Where will you store them?

CLOSET ....

....

3

Cook a week's worth of food in advance and defrost a meal nightly. I know you're heading home eventually; wouldn't it be great (barring another who's done this for you) to know dinner just needs heating up?

What 3 meals can you easily prepare and have enough for leftovers? SHRimP

....

....

What food items or supplies do you need on a shopping list of staples that can be used and stored long term?
ScALLoPS, TURKEY Hot DOGS ....

....

Hire someone to clean; your time is worth more. And that's a lesson allowing me to type this while the house is becoming spic 'n' span (and believe me - a pro does this much better than I ever have!)

4 ✓

From whom can you get a recommendation for this service?

....

....

Car pool. Just think of the added moments of sleep, conversation, brainstorming, creativity or ultimately, years to your life with this one!

5

Who's going your way and would like to share the driving?

....

....

Schedule appointments within a natural, logical driving pattern.

6 ✓

Need I really say more here?

....

....

Claim your free gift valued at $ 250.00 here: www.morefreetimezone.com/gift

7 Organize and label everything - files, drawers, folders, cabinets. It's really ok to give yourself a break with good organization and a professional layout; you never know just who will be impressed with your process perfection and the impact it might have.

Whose environment always seems neat and organized?

Dad , weekly clean office

How do they do it? (You'll want to ask before filling in this one.)

8 Hire a dog walker or kitty sitter. If the needs of your beloved furry family members prevent you from doing important activities - like taking vacations or other travel - maybe you need to rethink your priorities.

What responsible local person would do well in this task and would enjoy the role?

Who do you know whose animals are lovingly handled with the aid of another person?

9 Have a gardener (or teenager) water the plants and posies. I'm open to another point of view on this one as gardening could actually be a form of refreshment and creativity for you. However, if it becomes a burden, let it go. And don't ever forget to stop and gaze or sniff the wonder of your outdoor color.

Whose garden always looks great and could point you in the right direction? *Frank*

....

....

Don't have the money for these great ideas? Barter. It's amazing how willing people are to engage in these kinds of arrangements; if it provides a service the other party considers of value and/or it will allow you to pursue more meaningful tasks, then find your partner and do si do!

10

Who offers the services you need and would consider trading for services you offer?

....

....

Place daily needed papers and materials close at hand. Don't tell me walking to get them is your only form of exercise; that's just too lame in the face of reduced time to accomplish work!

11

Which 5 items do you reach for every day?

....

....

Where's the most logical location for them?

....

....

Don't fill anything to capacity - calendar, purse, drawer. Things are quicker to find with space between them and that's the point, isn't it?

12

And here it is, blank space with nothing to fill in...

....

....

13   Turn off the TV and exercise your mind; not only will you free up time to attend to what's more meaningful or talk with your family, you'll wake up some brain cells!

What time of day is ideal to have a conversation with available, at-home family members?   7 PM DINNER

....

....

14   Visit the doctor yearly. Health reduced by inattention robs us of more than time - we lose joy and opportunity.

When did you last have a physical exam?   1/30/19

....

....

And where is the doctor's phone number?   i PHone

....

....

15   Find a salon/spa you enjoy for hair, nail, body and skin care. While this initially adds tasks to your day, over time you'll discover the scheduled focus on yourself will allow for greater concentration and reduced stress - both necessary for more effective use of time. And who says they're not consistent with your priorities?

Your own example goes here. How could Chapter 1: "Having a Life" work for you?

① Say 'no'
② Printer ink
③ Scallops, shrimp, turkey hot dogs
④ Clean office on Friday
⑤ Someone to weed garden - Frank, Jose?
⑥ 7PM dinner. Turn off TV

What's your story? How will things change when you've implemented Tips from Chapter 1: "Having a Life"?

Less stress

Chapter 2

A Little Personal Development

Examples of how this could work for you:

The wrong legacy:

My client had inherited a business about which she had mixed feelings; while she became expert in the industry and dove in to be an active player, it didn't provide the feeling of accomplishment or self-expression critical to her self-image. During the time we worked together, the market conditions became ideal for her to sell her holdings and purchase other assets, more in keeping with her priorities and envisioned future. Making this transition was a difficult process. She had never felt secure in her own sense of personal direction, wasn't clear in the way she'd most enjoy business ownership and how it would add value to her life's dream. It took months for her to seriously look at the disconnect between her priorities and her daily routines. Eventually, she realized that her behavior, mostly driven by a business she despised, was taking precedence over her family which was her primary obligation. This serious review led to new commitments and actions, ultimately helping her to sell her business and embark on a new one, more in line with personal priorities.

Here's another story that might resonate with you:

A dedicated consultant with strong professional skills and personal ethics had affiliated himself with a more established firm as he began to build his own business. Over time he discovered the firm's service model and behaviors with clients was distressing and very unlike his own style of service delivery. However, he found it hard to break away; a sense of commitment to his colleague outweighed his sense of responsibility to himself. Therein lay the source of tremendous stress and the undermining of his ability to apply his talents in full measure. By learning to honor himself and his strongly held values, he broke away easily and, in the first completed year of his own practice, far exceeded the original goals for this new business. Articulating and believing in the benefits of a clearly envisioned future, both for self and family, were key components to the success of this engagement. This section is devoted to making that vision easier for you.

16 Learn how to ask for help. Why struggle with tasks at which you don't excel? Presidents do it; why not you? Get the help you need to complete work faster and with less stress. (Is this one tough? I know there are some for whom asking for help is a sign of weakness. If you fall in this category, a Bonus Gift is waiting for you at the end of the book. You'll never again struggle with the need to reach out and ask).

Who has the necessary skill and could help you with .... **?**

....

....

Claim your free gift valued at $ 250.00 here: www.morefreetimezone.com/gift

What is the cost to you if you don't get this done?

....

....

And what's your fear about asking for help with this?

....

....

Of the above two answers, which is worse to endure?

....

....

Schedule down time - it'll bring you back up. You deserve a break - for refreshment, new perspective, creative juices or a reward. Just schedule it at a natural break in your activity so you don't interrupt the flow of creative thinking.

17

What easy, brief relaxation could you schedule daily?
Breakfast, read paper, gym

....

Will you put it in your calendar? I'll wait......

Listen - you'll learn more quickly. You know that old cliché about having one mouth and 2 ears to be used proportionately? Pay attention by listening rather than talking; it will help you learn, understand, accomplish faster and with greater meaning.

18

With whom do you tend to commit the sin of not paying attention? Vicky, Woody, TAB board

....

....

What would you have learned more quickly if you listened with greater focus? Sale assistant

....

....

And how much time would you have gained as a result?
8 hrs/wk ....

....

19 Don't try to remember anything; write it all down. When you're assaulted with so many messages daily, the mental file cabinets get messy easily. Why try to remember and possibly do it badly? Write down (or record) important tasks, obligations and such; they'll get done right the first time, in less time.

Until you pick the journal or tool that works for you, here's your first opportunity to get into the habit:

Eureka moment I had last night before falling asleep
Co-lab / ULC Robotics Tour Designatronics ....

....

Brainstorm I had when writing an email

....

....

Great idea I saw at the dry cleaners that we could adapt

....

....

Now keep it going - get that journal or pocket recorder...
Use iPhone message recorder ....

....

Prepare: agendas, itineraries, calendars; don't do anything on the fly except create. With preparation, you have an opportunity to think through the process at hand, minimizing the likelihood of mistakes and forgotten needs and you'll speed completion of everything.

20

Friday, the 13, 2 p.m.   2/15/19, ~~march~~ agenda   2018 budget

....

....

By October 31

....

....

By the end of this fiscal cycle

....

....

Forgive yourself and others - NOW. You may not immediately see the relevance to time but believe me, bad feelings take up space where productive creativity could be. Let it go.

21

It's time to forgive; who?   Jamie

....

....

Forgive yourself here for: Jason's frgts

....

....

Chase nothing - good things will come your way when you know your priorities and focus your energy on achieving and enjoying them.

22

What have you been so frantically pursuing that's getting in the way of succeeding at other worthy pursuits? New business

....

....

23 Give up guilt and regret - use the opportunity to learn and improve, instead; won't that speed the goals you seek? Like the inability to forgive yourself, these emotions will hold you back from the progress and more satisfying emotions and projects life has waiting for you. Why give them the power to do this?

What one thing consumes you with guilt or regret?

....

....

How can you either resolve the issue or re-frame it (see it in another light) to find a more positive relationship with this thing that's eating at you?

....

....

If you're able to let go of these paralyzing emotions, what new opportunities will present themselves that previously were hidden from you? Whatever you write here, isn't it far better to enjoy than the corrosive pain of your guilt?

....

....

24 Develop boundaries and maintain them. The lack of boundaries is an easy invitation to misunderstanding, conflict and a slowing down of general progress in relations. Know your line in the sand and communicate it clearly to others.

What behavior or language would overstep your boundaries? Dishonesty

....

....

And who's often guilty of this, slowing down progress or taking up mental space?

....

....

How can you communicate to this person that the behavior is not acceptable to you?

....

....

What's stressing you? Talk about loss of time! Figure it out and get it out of your life - with healthy options, conversations that resolve (like the one you'll have in #24) and priorities that are honored by smart choices.

25

What's keeping you up at night that needs to be addressed so you can move forward?

....

....

Get enough sleep, eat well and maintain physical fitness. Come on; you've heard this your whole life; are you doing it yet? Well, here's another good reason: you'll approach time stealers with a refreshed, new approach and find ways to delegate, speed or abdicate their needs.

26

What one thing can you change today that will begin to improve your health? Avoid coffee, sugar

....

....

27   Tolerate nothing. Why be held hostage to frustration and disappointment? Let your own needs and values take precedence over others' bad behaviors.

What are you tolerating that slows down your ability to focus on what's truly meaningful for you?

....

....

28   Resolve problems quickly - don't waste time being angry. See #25, 27, 30 - these are all wasted uses of your emotional life and only serve a purpose when you find resolution, deeper meanings and stronger relations.

Start out with an easy one; what minor problem has been taking a disproportionate degree of your energy yet could be solved with one well-planned conversation? Cassidy

....

....

29   Give up your search for perfection. You'll only find procrastination and unfinished, nagging projects. Reach for what's right given the situation and opportunity it represents. You'll find your attention produces what's truly perfect in the moment - far more satisfying!

Which project has been unending because you just can't recognize it's done?

....
....

What has been delayed because you can't get this other project off your desk or mind?

....
....

Let go of relationships that are toxic and produce no results beyond stress and displeasure. A world of time for people you love will become available.

30

Can you think of someone who doesn't add to your life and to whom it's time to say 'so long'?

....
....

Ensure your basic needs have been met. Without having them in place, you're searching for what must be had before you'll find time for what you want.

31

What basic needs are not yet satisfied?

....
....

How does this lack keep you from moving forward and developing?

....
....

32 Be clear about the goals you pursue. Are they yours or goals others have urged upon you? Tying yourself to activities that honor others' priorities will detract from pursuit of your own values.

What goals are you pursuing that don't seem to ring your bells anymore (if they ever did)?

....

....

Whose goals are these really?

....

....

33 Acknowledge the truth about time: its passage has more to do with your thoughts and response to it than with a ticking clock.

Imagine this situation:

Two friends make a date to meet for lunch. One arrives on time and awaits the second who arrives 10 minutes late. While waiting, the first guest uses the time to read, confirm a next appointment, review emails, the menu or plan a later project. The second friend, en route yet delayed in traffic, is growing anxious about being late and can think of nothing else. The same 10 minutes passed yet each of these two people has experienced it completely differently because of their emotional response to time.

Make peace with the past and let go of what can no longer be altered. Only your response can be changed; is your response helping or hindering your progress?

34

What past event still rules your emotions?

....

....

Is this truly benefitting you?
How can you finally put it to rest and truly move forward?

....

....

Your own example goes here. How could Chapter 2: "A Little Personal Development" work for you?

① Use iPhone message recorder
② Prep agenda for Hit meetings
③ Avoid caffeine, sugar
④ Discuss pay w/ Cassidy

What's your story? How will things change when you've implemented Tips from Chapter 2: "A Little Personal Development"?

free up more time

Chapter 3

Now, Let's Take Care of Business

Examples of how this could work for you:

See yourself in this story?

In 2008 one of my small business clients told me that a goal for the year was to start taking off every Friday by June 1st. By focusing on delegation, hiring the right people who saw themselves as part of a team with opportunities for personal growth and reward, it happened. In 2009, as the recession worsened that same client told me his goal for the year was to have no daily responsibilities any longer. This, despite losing by mid-year 25% of his business. And yet, by learning the value of using time for the big picture needs of the business, it happened and sales continued to grow strongly.

Claim your free gift valued at $ 250.00 here: www.morefreetimezone.com/gift

Shift happens:

Wanting to create a second company to produce a service for which she had real enthusiasm, this client was unable to tear away from the daily routine of her current enterprise, which was running well and growing. She couldn't imagine having a role in which her primary function was big picture envisioning, strategizing and seeing the future. In her mind, if she couldn't see the activity she was engaged in, it wasn't a legitimate business activity. It was a hard concept to swallow; she'd felt that making product and overseeing its departure to customers was the most important thing she did. While she searched for the ideal person to take on the role of steering the new company, she came to see that her true role was building a business, not the business' product. She realized she was the ideal candidate to steer the new business and that the current enterprise could manage without her.

Finding the More Free Time Zone:

This client built a successful business that she loved and often couldn't believe how easily the money was flowing in. Yet, taking a day off here and there was a hard thing for her to do without feeling guilt. Within 6 months of us working together, she found a way to do so weekly, sometimes putting a fake appointment in her calendar to justify her absence. The test came when an employee expressed concern over a rumor: all the time my client spent out of the office appeared to be a sign that she was getting ready to sell. Her response of: "I earned this time" came without any sense of guilt; a great breakthrough!

Delegate everything that can be done by others and nothing that can be done only by you. When you take time to engage in tasks that can be done by others, you're losing the opportunity to profit from the work that only you can do. As a result, the benefit you might enjoy from envisioning, nurtured relationships, strategic alliances, and planning will take much longer to enjoy. Stop working below your pay grade!

35

What can you delegate? *I invoicing / monthly reports?*

....

....

Who's going to get this task? *Sarah?*

....

....

Empower your staff to think and decide. Until you take this step, you'll continue to be plagued by the unwanted, unnecessary interruptions from employees afraid to take action without you. You'll continue to be necessary to the day to day operation of your business processes – as the owner, that's not your job – and you won't be able to delegate.

36

Who needs clarity about the authority they have?

....

....

What level of authority do they have and how will that free you up?

....

....

Claim your free gift valued at $ 250.00 here: www.morefreetimezone.com/gift

37 Have systems in place and use them. Without systems, you can't provide consistency, either in your product or in your customers' experience. And, without systems, you're a slave to employees who may leave and take critical knowledge with them. Without systems, people can't learn, can't cross-train and can't take a day off – that's you, too!

Which business process needs to be systematized first? (i.e. marketing, accounting, product development, sales, training, budgeting, strategic planning, human resources – you get the picture.)

marketing, Update sales scripts

Whose help is necessary to ensure the full system is captured?

Jillian ? Aaron ?

38 Document processes so others can learn and do without you. Did you read #37? This step comes first; and to ensure your processes are completely documented, give them to a stranger and see how well they do with the process!

What technique is best for this job?

Who, other than you, is best suited to get this done?

39 Find partners to share the load. Very often you know someone engaged in the same work – or who needs the identical assistance – for which you're searching. If you share, you'll gain an ally, find time to do other activities and perhaps learn a new way to tackle the routine.

Who do you know who's been looking for the same resource you are?   TAB ?

....

....

Who do you know who's targeting the same audience as you, with a non-competing product that would be a natural companion to your own?

....

....

Have trusted advisors who've been there before to guide you through the unexpected or uncertain. So often, we call on past routines to handle things. When something non-routine crops up, you may have nothing in your memory bank to call on. That's one of the reasons you want to reach out to others – especially those not in your industry – who'll shorten the time you need to find a solution and perhaps one that might have never entered your mind.

40

Who are your trusted advisors, people who think differently than you do, and whose opinion you respect?   TAB
woody

....

....

Don't accept others' urgencies as yours – let others' monkeys stay on their shoulders and not jump to yours! This will happen a lot more easily if you handle #36 – teach them to think and decide up to some level of authority that will reduce their need to knock on your door.

41

Who needs to learn to solve their own problems before asking for your help?

....

....

How will you get this done?

....

....

How many fewer interruptions will you enjoy as a result?

....

....

42 Start with the end in mind; knowing your destination makes picking a path easier and more effective.

What's your desired outcome with a particular project or plan you're working on?

....

....

43 Make yourself replaceable – and then move on. When only you can handle all that must be done, you're prevented from growing into your more productive self and are a slave to your business. Ironically, the more we can let go of the sense of control that comes from this state, the freer we become.

Who's ready to move up the ladder? Aanra

....

....

What higher level work will you be able to do when s/he's trained?

marketing ....

....

Learn to trust that others know what they're doing. If you want to fulfill the suggestion in #43, here's a good place to start. They may not do tasks just as you would yet if the results are comparable or better, it may be worth more in the gain of a capable, accountable team than in the loss of 'my way or the highway'.

44

Who always gets the work done, even though you complain they're not following your style?

....
....

Be open to other ways than your own. Sounds a lot like #44 however, when we experience this bit of a mental shift, we open ourselves to a broader range of outcomes, any one of which might represent true opportunity for gain.

45

What have you resisted trying because you've "always done it this way"?

....
....

Stop doing errands. I challenge you.

46

What can you hand off to others who are better suited to these tasks?

....
....

Schedule free time – you need it and it deserves more than being just an interruption to some other activity. Give your free time your full attention and you'll easily discover why you want more of it; great motivator!

47

At what 2 times each day will you schedule a 15-minute break?

8 am - gym

6:30 pm - news

48

Don't schedule more than 65% of each day – you never know what opportunity – or emergency - may show up that wants your attention. And won't you be glad you can give it without compromising other obligations or plans?

Find this suggestion shocking?

It could be you're uncomfortable with the idea of having 're-serve' or available space. My theory on women's hand bags comes in here: no matter what size purse a woman carries – whether an elegant, palm-sized evening clutch or an over-sized book bag – it will magically get filled to the brim with the necessities and not-so necessities. We have a tendency to be uncomfortable with 'excess capacity'; it seem wasted. Instead, consider that 'capacity' as a necessary asset for the focused business owner, always prepared for the unexpected opportunity or challenge. Go ahead, try it beginning with next month's calendar.

49

Don't let anyone interrupt your flow – each 1-minute interruption will take 18 to reclaim the momentum you lost; no kidding. That 1-minute break will disrupt the flow of thought you had and you'll lose far more than what you might have gained with that ill-timed break.

Have a door? Close it. Draft your 'do not disturb' notice here:

No door? Practice saying a version of this:
"I can't speak with you now; I've got 3 p.m. or 10 tomorrow;
which works for you?"

Temporarily, you'll still lose focus however you'll be training
the interrupter against future, similar sins.

Keep your focus; what you planned to do is more important
than what others want to distract you with.

50

See #49 above and pair it with a slow withering glare; who
deserves to see it first?

....

....

Turn off your email program and install an auto response
message about when writers can expect your reply. If you can't
bear the withdrawal pains, at least start by turning off the
sound. Ready to turn it off? Here's your scratch pad for your
'vacation' or 'auto response' message:

51

'Thank you for your message; I'm committed to replying to
you within .... hours. If this is critical however, please
reach me immediately here: ....

....

Group together similar activities. It's much easier and more
productive to sequentially engage in tasks that call on similar
thought or behavioral activities.

52

Which 3 routine events make sense to schedule together?

....

....

How much time will this free up for you?

....

....

53 Connect the dots; are the things in which you're engaged serving a purpose or are they busy work?

Pick 3 items from your weekly routine and answer the above: are they purposeful for you or busy work? (and, if you can't tell the difference, consider checking in with your value system and priorities).

....

....

54 When working with documents, complete their function and file away – not at the bottom of another 'to do' pile on your desk or desk-top screen. You know which ones I'm talking about, right? We don't need to list them here. But if it's easier, I'll let you list them. Perhaps acknowledging their category on the page will make it harder for you to hide them in future:

Which documents/invoices/statements/etc. do you have a tendency to procrastinate completing? eue

....

....

55 Cut through the extraneous and get to the real matter quickly. Have a trusted assistant who reads through your mail or submitted reports and highlights the portions of concern to you for faster completion.

Don't have a trusted assistant? How much time and money are you losing each day as a result?

Schedule actual breaks so that, rather than interrupt yourself in the midst of a project, you stop at a natural, expected point. The unexpected break or interruption of 'just one minute' loses worthwhile mental flow and energy – nearly 20 minutes worth!

56

Think you've seen this tip already? You're right; why do you think that is?

Use the phone instead of memos or emails. You'll reach your party – and resolution – more quickly.

57

Who should you call today because the personal interaction will generate more punch than an email might?

Resign from obligations that no longer serve a purpose for you. Give yourself permission to do this and who knows what radical opportunities may present themselves?

58

What one thing, if let go, would open up space for something you've not yet been able to achieve? ωDI

Keep track of your routine activities and prioritize. Spend your time engaged in what's important yet not urgent and you'll

59

avoid the stress of handling what's important AND urgent.

How much time each week do you work at tasks that are not urgent yet important?

i hour

How can you increase that?

60 Want to get serious? Give up the 'not important and not urgent' activities. #1 tells you how to handle these! Remember #53 – connect the dots!

OK, nobody's looking - just how much time does this category take up?

What are you avoiding or setting aside in favor of this 'are you nuts?' category?

61 Figure out your peak performance times. Maximize their effectiveness with the most activity and achievement.

What time of day are you generally most creative and energized?

After gym/breakfast 1030–1100

What projects would fit well with that frame of mind?

Budget, proposals, update scripts, call list

Plan everything – vacation, shopping, correspondence, social times, as well as business projects – and less will be forgotten or vying for your attention.

62

Start here: I plan to take a week or long weekend on these dates:

This is where I/we want to go:

This is who has to know immediately:

Maximize travel time. When driving, make phone calls (if you have a hands-free phone); on planes or trains, read, develop ideas, advance projects and plan.

63

These are the tools I need to make travel time more effective and never sacrifice safety:

Spend the bulk of your time engaged in those activities you love and for which you have a natural aptitude and the time

64

you use to complete tasks will decline. Your own enthusiasm will add pace and focus.

What are the tasks for which you have a natural aptitude?

Running meetings, sales

How would engaging in them more often provide more free time?

make more sales

65 Don't let boredom or distraction become a part of your life. You'll discover new pockets of time well spent.

How can you get control over these mental drains and use your brain, rather than have it abuse you?

66 Automate what you can. Machines love repetition; not so much your brain!

What tasks are done better by tools so you can get done what machines can't?

marketing ?

67 Use your lunchtime. Learn, read, plan, follow up on projects, enjoy the company of those who you rarely see.

What one book, magazine or report have you been meaning

to read yet haven't?

....

....

Who can you invite to lunch next week who would add to your life, attitude or creativity?

....

....

Don't put up with loud noise and other distractions when working. It will cut down on your effectiveness; find a way to maximize the contribution of your workspace to help you focus – you spend so much time there!

68

What 3 things can you add or detract from your workspace to make it more inviting and productive for you?

....

....

Keep a list of all passwords and user names in one convenient and secure location. I know you know why.

69

Just how many lines would that require here?

....

....

Leverage all you do to maximize the value of time spent producing it the first time. For example: email content can become a blog post, can become an article, can become a 'white paper' give-away, can become a workshop, can become a 'home study' program, can become a competition, can become a group program – or a Tips book.

70

Name two projects you've produced that have more juice in them:

....

....

How?

....

....

71 Set up an automated billing system for recurring payments. Why spend time, and stamps, repeating what a bank can do for you?

Which recurring bills can you set up by automated deductions?

....

....

72 Fire your least profitable or most demanding clients. Or at least institute a 'heartburn fee'. It's likely that these customers are using an inappropriate amount of your time, given the reward to you; what's the value for you in this?

OK - no one's looking; name 2 you wish you could fire:

....

....

If it can't be done now, how will you increase the reward or opportunity you get from devoting more time to their needs?

....

....

73 Learn to hire the best person for the job; not the person who'd be most interesting to have around. Remember to evaluate

candidates from the job's perspective, not yours; keep in mind the likely result if you don't (that would be #74).

What does the job need to be done well?

....
....

Who's really a good judge of that?

....
....

If it's too late to address #73, then fire quickly – you'll save months of lost productivity and lost opportunity on the employee who's not the right fit for you.

74

What needs to be done first?

....
....

Join or establish a mastermind or other peer advisory group. You'll add to the range of creative ideas available to you from perspectives other than your own from people who've no personal stake in the outcome except wanting you to succeed.

75

Who might be interested in joining this venture?

....
....

Let others know how they can step up to handle more tasks. Employees want to know they're contributing to the company (and to their own) success so position 'more tasks' as 'more responsibility' and you'll have accomplished two important results.

76

Who's ready for this one?

....

....

77 Arrange for employees or team members to gradually take on more responsibility. What perfect timing! This is ideal now that you've decided to take on #76.

What benchmarks will you set to assess their progress?

....

....

What reward will you enjoy for having delegated wisely?

....

....

78 Periodically review your priorities vs. your routines. If they're not consistent you're adding a measure of stress and engaging in the unimportant. Not only are you slowing down results, you're taking time from what's more profitable for you. Use suggestions in the Personal Development section to be more consistent with what you value.

What 3 routines seem to have lost all meaning and value for you?

....

....

When will you let them go?

....

....

Claim your free gift valued at $ 250.00 here: www.morefreetimezone.com/gift

Find a salon/spa you enjoy for hair, nail, body and skin care or body work. While this initially adds an activity to your day, over time you'll discover the scheduled focus on yourself will allow for greater concentration and reduced stress – both necessary for more effective use of time. And who says they're not consistent with your priorities? And, don't think this is a Tip for women, only!

79

You've seen this Tip before. And just why is it here again in the Business Section? I'll let you answer that one:

....

....

Write down (or record with a small pocket recorder) your thoughts, observations, fleeting ideas. It's too hard to remember the brief moments of inspiration we want to flesh out when the time is right. And you want to reinforce your mind to be open to new possibilities that you'll pursue when you're in the More Free Time Zone.

80

Start here and then get an attractive journal that you won't lose! Great idea of the moment that you can implement for your benefit today:

....

....

How do you feel? Really, I'm asking. Undetected or unidentified sources of stress can detract from your ability to get things done and will slow you down. Deal with the upset that's distracting you and you'll find speed of completion is just one great result.

81

How is your general mood affecting your ability to move through your day smoothly?

....

....

82 Remember why you're doing it all. Focus on what will be gained with the free time you're seeking and your mind will start to think in terms of available space for you to move forward.

All right, what is the real payoff for you?

....

....

83 Shift away from comfortable routines. By shaking up a usual schedule you'll be forced to re-think tasks and why you continue to pursue them. You'll also find new ideas and relationships that add 'oomph' to the doing.

Anything come to mind?

....

....

84 Associate completion of a task with a desirable reward. Whether you choose massage, jewelry, concert tickets or a luxury getaway is less relevant than the fact that you want it – bad. Great motivation to get it going and get it done!

If you complete .... *by* .... *your reward will be:*

....

....

Break every large project into small, manageable portions that can be completed within a day. Otherwise the overwhelm of the bigger task may prevent you from starting and you'll slow down your progress.

85

Consider a project that's due in 2 months; what smaller increments can be accomplished daily that move you closer to completion?

....

....

Define your sense of 'enough'. You may discover it's already found you and there's no need to spend time acquiring more; how much time will that open for you?

86

What have you always wanted to achieve that, in fact, you already have and perhaps didn't realize?

....

....

How will the acknowledgement of that achievement open up time, space and opportunity for you?

....

....

Surround yourself with people who don't think as you do. You'll expand your range of possible solutions with different perspectives and will speed the discovery of new outcomes.

87

Who do you generally avoid because they never see things as you do?

....

....

How might having them around become an advantage for something you're wrestling with?

....

....

88   Before choosing an activity, ask: what's worth pursuing now? Connect available time with your priorities and your natural energy will make things run more smoothly, productively and quickly.

What's truly the most valuable thing – just for you - that you could attend to now?

....

....

89   Be in the present – focusing on past regrets and future anxieties robs you of the sense of pleasure and achievement to be gained right now and sloooows yooouuu dowwwwnnnn.

Check in with your gut: where's the upset coming from (and I don't mean lunch)?

....

....

How can you address it so it doesn't eat time?

....

....

90   Forget the nonsense that you work better under pressure. Too much stress is ultimately a killer. Activities pursued under stress allow the details to just be glossed over or ignored, resulting in added work and more time needed to get it done - again.

What physical activity will let the tensions out? Racquet ball? Massage? A long walk? You pick and then schedule one:

....

....

Procrastination may be the result of some underlying discomfort with the project you face; examine what's getting in the way, discuss with others and move forward.

91

Why are you really avoiding getting X done?

....

....

Always, always be willing to ask for help. Are you afraid of how a request for help makes you sound? A bonus gift is at the end of the book so you'll never fear using this strength again.

92

What could I really use help getting done or out of the way?

....

....

Who's really good at this that I could ask?

....

....

Cancel subscriptions to publications and e-news that no longer fit your priorities yet make you feel obligated to give them your attention. Take another look at #53.

93

What do I delete or trash without ever reading it?

....

....

Claim your free gift valued at $ 250.00 here: www.morefreetimezone.com/gift

94

Do you use a paper calendar? CRM data base tool? Smart Phone? The important word here is what you 'use'; don't select your scheduling tool because it's what's recommended – select the tool you'll use, over and over again; now that you're scheduling everything, this is critical to getting more free time.

What's it going to be?

....

....

95

Set and manage others' expectations. Make sure all parties to a plan understand their part and your part in its completion. Great communication is essential to finding free time.

Who do I need to clue in to my current plans?

....

....

Who needs to communicate with me or the team about their progress?

....

....

96

Don't solve other people's problems. You do no one any favors and you'll soon find yourself resenting the person you assisted for diverting your attention away from your own priorities.

Who needs to learn how to solve their own problems?

....

....

Schedule time to dream, envision, plan and think. You'll accomplish so much more when you work with your brain instead of your hands. This is what 'excess capacity,' mentioned in #48, is made for!

97

My best 'dream time' is (same time each day or week, please):

....

....

Feel like your timing's always off or you're never getting the benefit of 'luck' with your plans? It could be you're missing the 'gut' clues about opportunities that always work in the favor of those whose timing is perfect; start paying closer attention to what your body is telling you about luck and timing. Maybe #99 will give you the mental focus, and body awareness, to use this asset.

98

When do you seem to be most in touch with your physical or emotional self?

....

....

What's generally going on then?

....

....

Being in the present may cost you time if in the present you're enduring difficult emotional circumstances. Parse it down to the smallest moment of time as in: 'at this moment, I'm reading this and nothing else is happening'. That kind of pinpoint focus will remove the upset of other circumstances happening in the background and delaying completion of this task. Be here, now.

99

Read that last one again and focus. There's nothing else to do; it's a great exercise to speed comprehension, interpretation, and practical application.

100

Be aware of your own standards. Standards are those levels of behavior we expect from ourselves as a measure of excellence. If you find you're compromising your standards you may be sacrificing excellence that will require time to correct.

What business-related standards have I let go in favor of expediency?

....

....

How have I, or the business, suffered as a result?

....

....

101

Now and then, your timing will be off; accept it, move on and learn. Now go do.

What's first?

....

....

Your own example goes here. How could Chapter 3: "Now, Let's Take Care of Business" work for you?

What's your story? How will things change when you've implemented Tips from Chapter 3: "Now, Let's Take Care of Business"?

Just One More Thing...

O k, you've read all these Tips, you've tried a number of them and even with days of more free time, you're still occasionally engaged in tasks for which your engine just won't hum. It happens. In those instances, your spirit may need a 'lift' to get you in the More Free Time Zone. Try this: before engaging in projects that are necessary and for which you have no love – and which can't easily be delegated – find that ritual behavior or thought process that may help shift you into a zone of effectiveness or flow: your favorite music, preferred beverage, plants, art or photos that lift your positive, creative spirit. Turn off all tools that beep and whistle (unless attached to you for medical reasons).

In other words, make your work environment as attractive and supportive as possible; think of it as your sanctuary and it will support you through even the most tedious of projects – like figuring out just how to delegate this one!

Claim your free gift valued at $ 250.00 here: www.morefreetimezone.com/gift

BONUS: #s 16 and 92 promised a bonus and here it is:

How to Just Reach Out and Ask for Help:

Do you have moments when you recognize you'd benefit from getting help yet are afraid the request will convey some flaw or weakness on your part? You're about to be cured! Answer this: when someone asks for your help because they acknowledge your expertise in some area AND you're in a position to say 'yes' without adding a dose of stress to your own schedule, how does it make you feel? Pretty nice, right? Not only has your skill been acknowledged, you've also been able to come to the aid of another and help them move forward through a rough time. It's as if they gave you a gift while, at the same time, got the solution they needed. So, how about you offering a gift in exchange? Reach out and ask for help from someone who has the skill or resource to assist you. Not only will you get the solution you were worried about, you'll have also given a gift to another.

So, ask for help, right now, and make someone feel good. Need help figuring out how to best use all the additional time you found with these Tips? Here's my contact info; ask me for help and I'll enjoy receiving your gift!

Andrea Feinberg

andrea@coachinginsight.com
www.morefreetimezone.com

It's great here in the Zone! Stop by, anytime.

Appendix

Mind Benders for New Perspective

Space,
The Final Frontier

I'm a trekkie - I know what the "T" stands for in Captain James T. Kirk, I know where he was born and how he cheated his way through the Star Fleet Space Academy exam. I know who was the first Captain of the Star Ship Enterprise (not Kirk!), the inspiration for my cell phone's Blue Tooth device and that my first cell phone (the Motorola Star Tac) was originally Kirk's crew's communicator. I also know the Prime Directive that guided every mission and alien encounter: Starfleet's General Order #1, the most prominent guiding principle of the United Federation of Planets says there can be no interference with the internal affairs of other civilizations.

Do you know your "Prime Directive"?

Do you know the over-riding vision for your life that pulls you forward daily, one that helps guide your decisions and choices? Sometimes we get caught up in the obligations we take on (or, even more challenging - we're overwhelmed by responsibilities that seem to find us without our active choice) and we forget that all choices, actions and affiliations must be consistent with a personal big picture, our own "prime directive". If we forget the fundamental importance of honoring that personal commitment, the direction in which we want to take our lives, the result tends to be a sense of going in circles. We feel we're not making progress, not getting closer to our own life purpose.

Small business clients frequently complain about this aspect of leading an enterprise: their business is taking them away from more personally fulfilling activities. I hear things like "This place would fall apart without me" or "No one else will get it done like I can". Whether or not this is true is irrelevant if you believe that it is true. And believing that it is may keep you traveling in small circles, a slave to a business (or other obligation) that may grow yet prevent you from enjoying the personal growth you seek, fulfilling your own 'prime directive' in the bigger picture of your life.

And so I'll ask again: do you know your own 'Prime Directive" - your vision for your life? When you do, the choices inherent in crafting a business, career or relationship are easier to make, clearer to follow and take you forward always, never in circles, never away from what's most personally meaningful. Take the time to consider your daily choices: are they consistent with the picture you have for your life? Will these activities pull you forward every day, forward toward the vision you hold for yourself?

If you haven't discovered the vision you have for your life, how will you know you're on the best possible path each day? There's no one around who'll yell out 'getting warmer!' to help pick directions. There's no one to whom you can say "set a course for my dreams, Mr. Sulu!"

There's you and there's the time you set aside to learn what's critically important to you, to acknowledge it and set your coordinates to get there. Because, while space is the final frontier, it's just not the space 'out there'. It's the space right here, within your heart and mind, where the greatest adventure is to be found.

Need a guide?

10 Tips For
Stress Reduction

and No, "Biting Your Nails" Doesn't Count

How many of us could say we've never encountered a stress-ful moment? (If you're a business owner, you're laughing at this one.) Certainly, only the very lucky, the very few. For the rest of us, we know all too well how the stress of change can lean on us and become our constant, unwanted companion. While we all know the signs of stress - anxiety, stomach knots, disorientation - did you know it can affect your immune system as well? Worse than that, our bodies don't know the difference between stress experienced and stressful situations recalled - the effect on our bodies is the same. So, the next time stress arises - and you may be feeling it right now - consider these few easy ideas to combat this unwanted state of being:

1. Consider your desired outcome - visualize what you want the end result to be and consider how to make it real.

2. Understand that the cause of the stress is temporary; it will pass. No matter how severe it may feel for you, in time all your systems will return to absolute normal.

3. You've already successfully navigated many challenges in your life. How did you do it? Consider which of these techniques can help your current situation.

4. Observe your language and the self-talk in your head. Does it look backward or forward? Add the context of positive possibility vs. forgone losing proposition. This is where that old phrase about a self-fulfilling prophecy is useful. As long as you are prophesying, make it a good one.

5. Stay focused in the present. Despite the sensation of being off balance or threatened, you are in this transition for a reason - look for the lessons in the process.

6. Seek support. Find at least one person who will really listen to you without judgment. The right family member, friend, or coach can support you through the process.

7. Take time for stress relief, relaxation techniques and good healthful living practices. Don't use the upset in part of your life as an excuse to abandon your healthy routines.

8. If it's comfortable for you, connect with your spiritual side. Use prayer, meditation or reflection on spiritual literature, or whatever works for you. In the written word you may find a companion in the writer whose experience mirrors your own.

9. Give up trying to control every aspect of the outcome. Realize that we never really know what will occur even in the next moment. Having visualized your intended outcome, take the actions that move you toward it and know that you will handle whatever materializes. Create a vision of success that pulls you towards it.

10. Remember: this transition does not represent your whole life. It may shock many areas of your life and through it all you will still be you. Trust that though it may take years, the outcome will be woven into the broad, rich journey of your unique life.

You Think Hiring One Employee is Tough?

What's it Like to Inherit a Company Full of 'Em?

W hat's your process for hiring? I'll bet you spend hours pouring over resumes, set a few appointments and have the promising candidates meet several decision makers before coming to a conclusion that their background, training and experience is just right. Yet, with that format, you're bound to make the mistakes that come with ignoring the 'soft' side of the employee: their behavioral style, attitudes, core beliefs and values that can have a real impact on performance. Now, imagine this hundreds of times over when you inherit a company full of unknowns with a single merger. Need a bottle of aspirin?

How can an astute company (with a willing and pro-active merger partner) reduce the risk of sinking their deal on issues they neglected to consider before they wrote the contract? I won't make you guess, here's the answer: statistically accurate, verified assessments are excellent tools for this purpose. Companies who routinely hire individuals for replacement or new positions are wise to benchmark the behavioral style or attitudes and values of the applicant who's best suited to fill the job. How do you know what the job really needs from the standpoint of 'soft skills'? With a benchmark profile in hand and relevant interview questions applied equally to all candidates, promising interviewees can then be assessed to see how closely they match the ideal. Of course, they must also have the requisite education, training and experience for the position.

Imagine then, if a company took its own profile, as a collective employer? The principals at the top would then be able to compare their corporate profile with that of their proposed partner. Compatible? Great! Not so compatible? Well, what does each company have to change or compromise to make this marriage work? Is it worth the effort? Can they quantify the cost of the added time necessary to bring the companies to cultural parity?

Imagine how much friction could be reduced with this pro-active stance! Just think of the impact this technique could have to speed the incorporation of two previously separate companies and all their new employee-colleagues. Imagine the enhanced speed of recouping the investment, enhanced productivity, reduced employee turnover. Can anyone find a way to help companies see the light? Probably have to put it clearly in dollars potentially gained or changed share price to make them hear because, so far, there's no bailout for mismatched corporate marriage partners.

Other Valuable Resources from Andrea Feinberg

to Have More Money, Enjoy Your Business and Love Your Life

30-Day Challenge to Get More Free Time

30-day e-class

www.morefreetimezone.com/30daychallenge/

The '30 Day More Free Time Challenge' is delivered to your e-mail box, every 3rd day for 30 days. Each of the 10 brief segments you'll receive will focus on a different type of time-related headache:

- planning too many events
- not inspired being at your desk
- allowing frequent interruptions
- hiring people who never get it right
- poorly planned & zero-result meetings
- getting blind-sided by the unexpected
- confusing being busy with being effective
- spending precious time on every priority except your own

Relief from these stresses will result in more free time. Complete the program, and find 1 hour of free time gained with every lesson. I promise, you'll have gained 10 hours of more free time within 30 days. However, at that point, you're just getting started because over time, as the effectiveness of each lesson really takes hold – for you and those you work with – you'll begin to see a continued, rolling effect of more and more free time. **$19.95**

Win with Your Hidden Assets

Build Your Business with the Treasure at Your Fingertips!

www.morefreetimezone.com/win-with-your-hidden-assets/

You possess a treasure chest of skills, assets, resources and talents that are waiting to be used by you. All are within your current personal or working environment. All can be leveraged to reduce costs and produce additional product, revenue stream, marketing benefits and occasionally, time off for you. This 14-session e-class, ready and delivered on your schedule, will help you identify under-used assets. Each discussion will help you see these treasures with 'new eyes' and discover their potential - greater benefit for you and your enterprise. The lessons and workbook will guide you to maximize these opportunities in ways that are uniquely appropriate for you and your business.

Wouldn't you like the key to opening your own personal treasure chest, capitalizing on the investment of time, energy and money you've already put into building your business?

Wouldn't you like to know that all your assets are working as hard and effectively as you are?

Claim your free gift valued at $ 250.00 here: www.morefreetimezone.com/gift

In this 14-lesson program, you'll discover at least 50 assets that could lead to greater productivity and reward for you and your business.

What Can You Expect to Gain?

- **maximized leverage** of your existing product, personnel, processes, relationships
- **enhanced profit** margin
- **greater contribution from fixed costs** (plant, personnel, utilities)
- a way to **invest energy instead of money**
- a means to **avoid the need for external funding** sources
- **improved communications** with your staff, vendors, customers
- **new sources of creativity**
- **expanded productivity**
- **more time for you**
- **in short, complete control of your business!**

Every 4 days you'll receive a lesson, worksheets and exercises to help you pinpoint the many opportunities for expanded benefit your hidden assets could provide. The lessons will show you how to re-frame your thinking about each element of your business. Each will include simple exercises to implement what you've learned. And, because I understand the kind of busy schedule you maintain, each day's activity requires no more than 1/2 hour.

This program makes no assumptions about the nature or size of your business; the results and suggestions will be completely customized to your situation. Whether you provide a service or product, **this system will work for you.**

Buy it now and start profiting immediately! **$29.95**

Claim your free gift valued at $ 250.00 here: www.morefreetimezone.com/gift

8 & ½ Tips to Out-Compete the Competition

8 & ½ Tips and Tools delivered in your e-box, 1 at a time

www.morefreetimezone.com/quality-time/

We all have competitors and respond to them in varied ways. You see them at industry events and share war stories or review trends. When they make a move, you parry with a competitive response; perhaps a price change, maybe a shift in marketing messages. Sometimes, while keeping your eyes on them, you're shifting attention away from the all-important customers you serve.

However, believe it or not, your competitors can be a huge source of tested and validated research when choosing your own next move with your business.

Want to learn how?

What Can You Expect to Gain?

With this program, you'll find ways to learn from your competitors - the good, the bad and the ugly. You'll enjoy an insider's experience with their policies, communications, long and short range planning. Get a new perspective on how to maximize industry opportunities and challenges. Each tip is designed to keep you informed about your industry, focused on your buying audience and ways to increase your value to them. Get a different perspective on successful marketing and customer service.

This program makes no assumptions about the nature or size of your business; the results and suggestions will be completely customized to your situation. Whether you provide a service or product, this system will expand the range of options available to nurture your relationship with your customers.

Bonus: Complete the program and receive a comprehensive listing of 300 resources to learn more about your competition.

Buy it now; start profiting immediately! **$8.95**

The Keys To Success
7 Steps to Success as You Define It!

www.morefreetimezone.com/quality-time/

Three months of coaching delivered by e-mail, 1 lesson each week; coaching lessons, reflections, resources and exercises to enjoy success on your terms!

Self-knowledge is the **KEY** to having the life and business you want. Understanding the priorities, values and intentions of your life are critical to enjoying consistency in all its areas: relationships, business success, health, spiritual and personal development. Sometimes when examining your deepest thoughts and feelings you may acknowledge you'll never reach your desired destination without making some change, perhaps using a different map, a different set of beliefs to guide you.

Acknowledging that change is necessary for growth and success (as you define it) is an important mental shift. This program is designed to help you determine if the map you're using (your attitudes, behaviors and assumptions) are consistent with the path you want to travel. And, if it isn't, it will guide you to a renewed perspective, one that honors your values and one that will support you as you move forward with renewed purpose.

The questions and activities you'll receive each week are designed to do two things:

- help you **clarify and articulate what's confronting you right now**
- help you **understand the big picture context** for the decisions and affiliations in your life

Each week, you'll receive a group of questions and exercises designed to illuminate these factors in your life or business. There are never any judgments here. No one will call you on your candor or its lack. Your true benefit will result from the honesty with which you confront yourself and put systems in place to help you with the changes you consider necessary.

The degree to which you're willing to take a close look in the mirror is the degree to which you'll be able to assess what needs to be changed and the degree to which you'll benefit from the process.

Start benefitting right now! Three months of weekly coaching, opportunities for change and support, delivered one week at a time. **$49.95**

Claim your free gift valued at $ 250.00 here: www.morefreetimezone.com/gift

"The Essential Coaching Book: Secrets to a Winning Life"

from the Professional and Personal Coaches of United Coaching Associates

This book was written with only a single goal: to help you identify your personal vision and enjoy a satisfying, successful life, on your own terms, no matter how you define "a winning life." A group of 15 professionally trained coaches share their knowledge, insights, and perspective. Each coach is knowledgeable and passionate about their area of expertise and each is here to support you. This book was written as a collaborative effort by members of United Coaching Associates.

Claim your free gift valued at $ 250.00 here: www.morefreetimezone.com/gift

Throughout this book, each coach is your partner as you work through the suggestions and exercises that resonate with you. Additionally, at the end of this book you'll find resources to continue the exploration of subjects most meaningful for you.

What Can You Expect to Gain?

- How to set your vision with concrete steps to get you there
- Specific chapters that guide you towards romance, career enhancement, inner growth, a well- run business, physical health, or a means to plan and enjoy the rest of your life
- Worksheets and exercises that will be meaningful throughout your life, companions to help see you through transitions and growth
- Resources to add to the knowledge you've learned for each topic explored in the book

Buy it now and find the partners, support and accountability to guide you through the changes you seek!

$18.95 plus sales tax, shipping

www.iuniverse.com/Bookstore/BookSearchResults. aspx?Search=The Essential Coaching Book

Raves from Fans of Time Junkie;

these people found their More Free Time Zone

"Andrea, this book is simply amazing! This is the first book I've found on using time effectively that doesn't tell me how to manage time - it guides me to manage myself smartly through time; and that's a lot easier to manage, especially when you make the real pay off so obvious and attractive."

Milana Leshinsky, Passive Income Coach, milana.com

......

"These tips are not the usual stale time management ideas that come from an old cookie cutter; they're fresh, pithy and I've already circled the first 10 I'm going to implement today."

John A. Hill, President /CEO
Long Island Advancement of Small Business

Claim your free gift valued at $ 250.00 here: www.morefreetimezone.com/gift

"Not one of these tips is designed to make me work faster or harder in what would be another failed attempt at 'time management.'"

Laura Wiletsky; President, Laura Wiletsky & Associates, Public Relations with Visible Results

......

"Time is that precious commodity that we never seem to have enough of. If only we could steal back some time each day, imagine what we might accomplish! Fortunately, Andrea Feinberg's "101 Ways to Get More Free Time" provides practical tips to help you take control of your time - and your life! As a creative type who is constantly jumping from project to project, I found the third section of the book, "Let's Take Care of Business," particularly helpful. Andrea's guide is loaded with ideas and actions steps that you can use immediately!"

Lou Bortone, "The Online Video Guy"
www.OnlineVideoBranding.com

......

"It's refreshing to read a book that truly provides a new perspective. You'll discover insights and learn practical tips that will help you transform your business management style for better business results and a more rewarding life. This book is a gem!"

Stephanie Leibowitz; President, Cultural "Insight"

Claim your free gift valued at $ 250.00 here: www.morefreetimezone.com/gift

"Andrea gets to the heart of time management through her insightful tips. Most books stop there. This one does not. Andrea takes each tip and creates challenging questions to help in their implementation. Brilliant!"

Jacquelyn Gernaey; CEO & Founder The Alternative Board New York

"This book benefits from having been written by a real long-time business owner whose perspective is right on the money! Andrea knows how busy we all are to learn new tricks or waste time re-visiting old, discarded ones. Bottom line — this book ROCKS!"

Craig Duswalt, Speaker and Creator of the 'RockStar System For Success', www.CraigDuswalt.com

"Andrea knows how busy we all are, and gives tips that certainly will help me to develop a much more effective approach to managing my time!"

Donna Rhodes Joseph
CEO, Rhodes-Joseph & Tobiason Advisors

"Every Tip here is an opportunity for me to manage my own actions within the time I've got available - a much more effective approach than trying to manage time!"

Carol Forgash, LCSW, BCD; Co-Director: The Lifeline Center; Editor/Co-Author: Healing the Heart of Trauma and Dissociation with EMDR and Ego State Therapy

Claim your free gift valued at $ 250.00 here: www.morefreetimezone.com/gift

"After reading the "101 Tips on How to Get More Free Time Now," it made me seriously think about the ways I try to maximize my free time - both personal and business. I recommend that you read Sections 1 & 2 on Personal Life and Personal Development since these areas lay the foundation for the Tips that lie ahead within the Business Section. As someone who had worked his entire career in corporate America, and has tried to improve my overall free time, I feel the business tips outlined are applicable for both people running a small business, as well as individuals managing a corporate business department. Once you read through the entire book, it should be reviewed from time to time in small doses as an ongoing tool, in order to maximize its usefulness and impact."

Jack Szluka, Sales Professional